MAZES 3

MAZES 3
BY VLADIMIR KOZIAKIN

GROSSET & DUNLAP
A NATIONAL GENERAL COMPANY
PUBLISHERS/NEW YORK

Dedicated once again
to my father
Piggy
and the Frog

Copyright © 1973 by Vladimir Koziakin
Published simultaneously in Canada

ISBN: 0-448-02064-5

Manufactured in the United States of America

INTRODUCTION

In the event that you have finished the first two volumes of mazes, here is the third collection of these graphic puzzles inspired by the labyrinths of Antiquity.

The solving of a maze puzzle is simple in the telling. Just take a pencil, plunge in where the arrow points, and work your way out without crossing any solid lines. If you get hopelessly lost you can consult the solutions in the back of the book. However, don't be bothered if your solution doesn't agree with the "official" one —some mazes have more than one way out and so long as you get out without crossing any solid lines, you're fine. If you wish to keep your maze free of pencil marks, try using a piece of tracing paper.

To make your meandering through the mazes more of a challenge, a rated time limit is given to each maze. Thus you can compete with yourself or with friends. But do remember that time is highly subjective. You may lope through one maze only to be hung up interminably on the next. Whatever happens, don't worry —even if you don't solve the maze within the time limit you won't be fed to the Minotaur.

For those of you who were traveling abroad or looking the other way the past two years, Mazes *and* Mazes 2 *are also available wherever fine books are sold.* Mazes *for children and less competitive-minded adults are also available under the title* Mazes for Fun.

Vladimir Koziakin

Maze 1

ANIMALCULUS

| Rated Time Limit | 2½ Minutes |

Maze 5

KINGFISHER

Rated Time Limit | 4½ Minutes

Maze 7

GRIFFIN

| *Rated Time Limit* | *6 Minutes* |

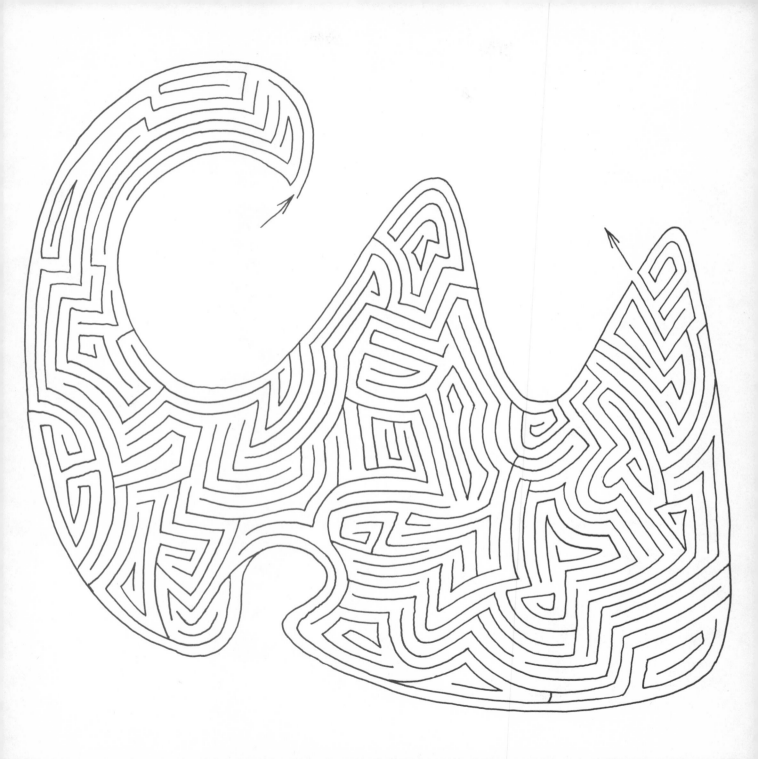

Maze 8

DODO

Rated Time Limit | *6 Minutes*

Maze 9

BOOMERANG

Rated Time Limit | 7 Minutes

ERMINE

| Rated Time Limit | 7 Minutes |

Maze 11

CRYSTAL

Rated Time Limit | 7½ Minutes

Maze 12

SOBERSIDES

Rated Time Limit | *8 Minutes*

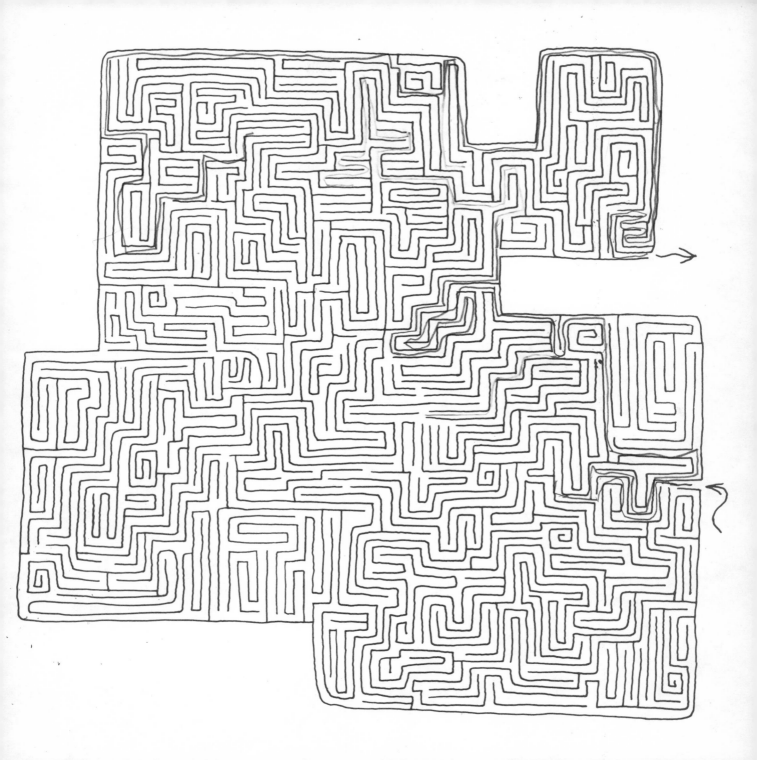

Maze 13

COBWEB

Rated Time Limit | 8½ Minutes

Maze 14
MODULE
| Rated Time Limit | 10 Minutes |

Maze 17

SQUAWK

| *Rated Time Limit* | *11 Minutes* |

Maze 18

HARLEQUIN

Rated Time Limit | *12 Minutes*

Maze 19
ZIGZAG
Rated Time Limit | 12 Minutes

Maze 20
DREAMS
Rated Time Limit | 12½ Minutes

FUNNY VALENTINE

| Rated Time Limit | 14 Minutes |

Maze 22

KISS

| Rated Time Limit | 15 Minutes |

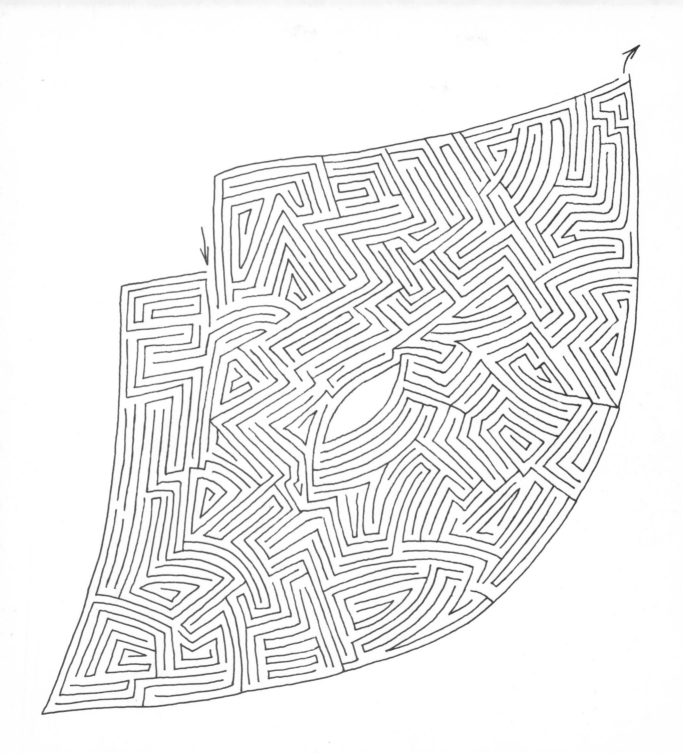

Maze 23

BAROOM!

| Rated Time Limit | 16 Minutes |

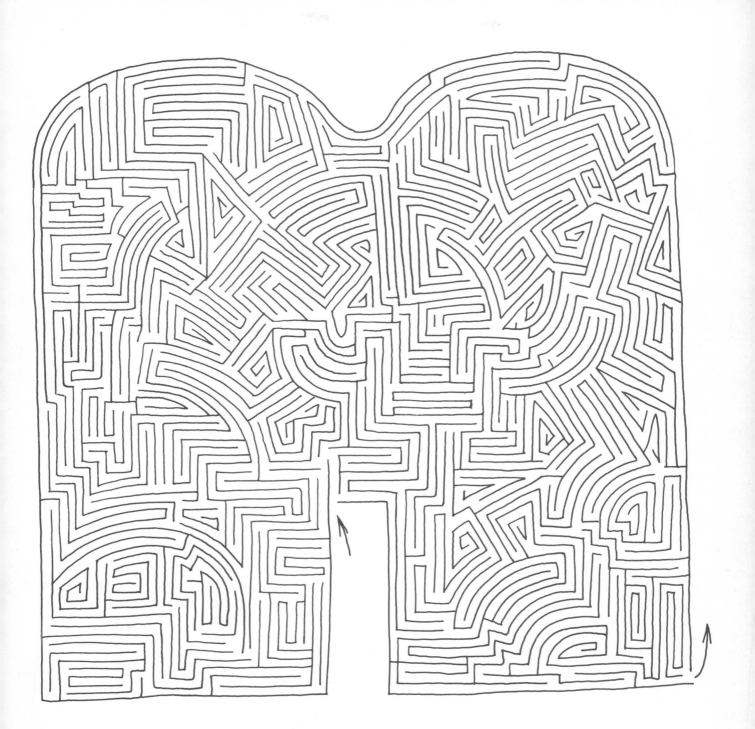

Maze 24

HORNED TOAD

Rated Time Limit | 18 Minutes

Maze 25

CARP

| Rated Time Limit | 20 Minutes |

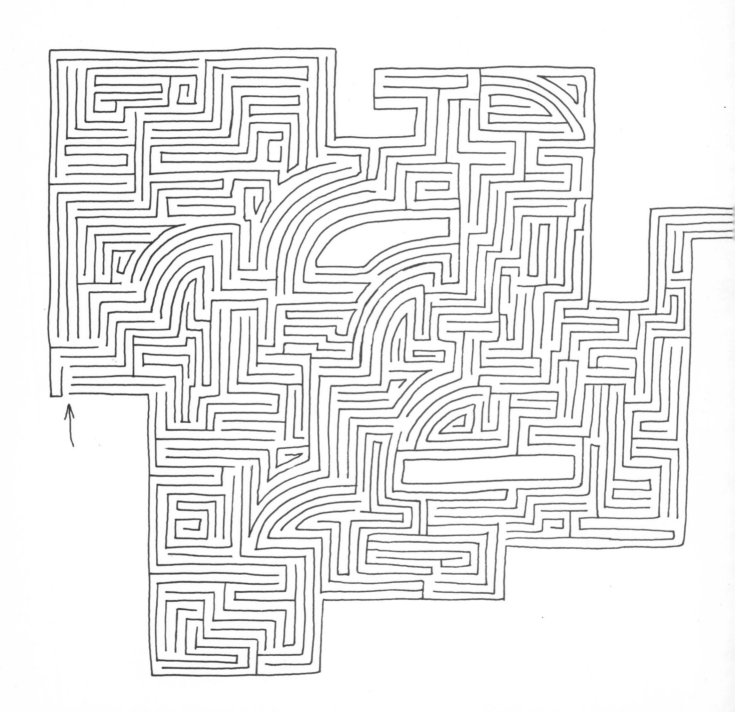

Maze 27
PROBOSCIS
Rated Time Limit | 24 Minutes

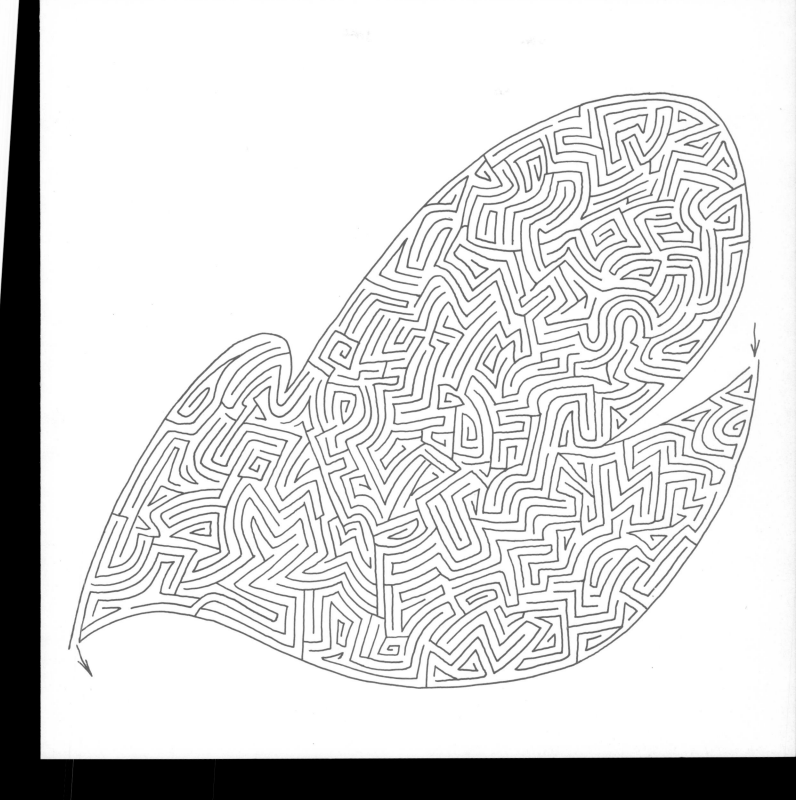

PERIPATETICUS

| Rated Time Limit | 25 Minutes |

Maze 29
WHIRLIGIG
Rated Time Limit | 27½ Minutes

JIGSAW PUZZLE

| Rated Time Limit | 30 Minutes |

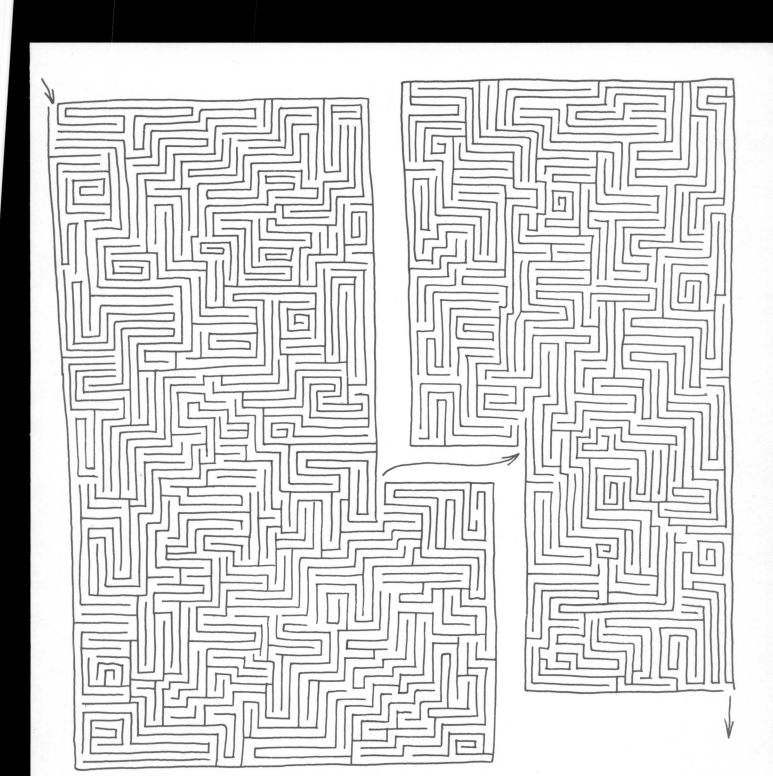

Maze 31

INTERCEPTOR

| *Rated Time Limit* | *32 Minutes* |

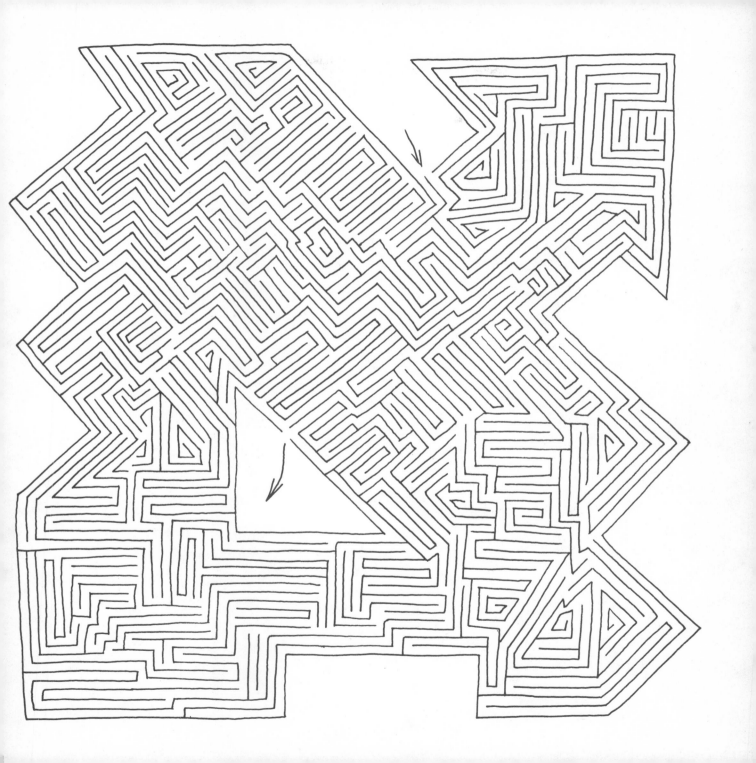

Maze 32

BLITZ

Rated.Time Limit | *33½ Minutes*

Maze 33

E FOR EFFORT

Rated Time Limit | 35 Minutes

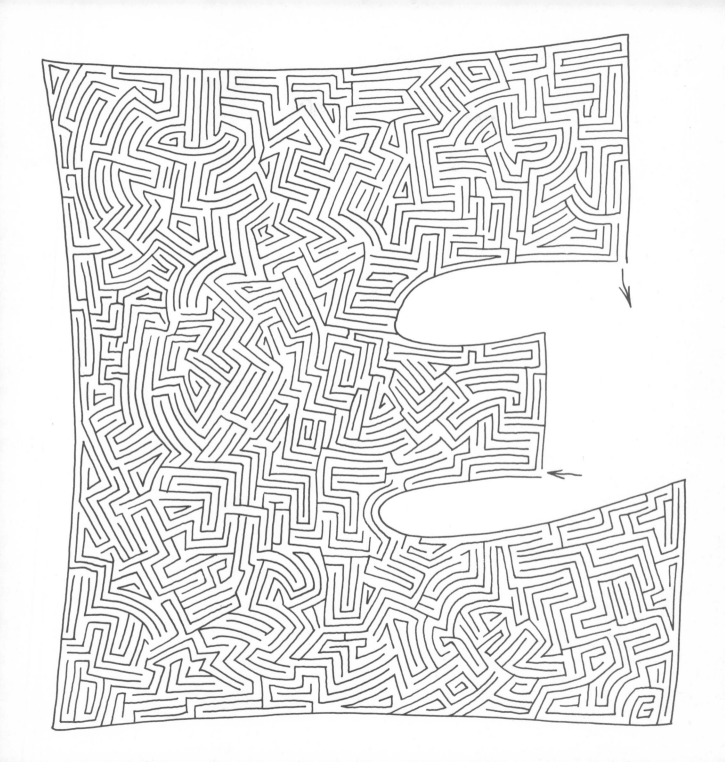

Maze 34

BLOWUP

Rated Time Limit | *36½ Minutes*

Maze 35

NAMBY-PAMBY

Rated Time Limit | 39 Minutes

ORBIT

| Rated Time Limit | 40 Minutes |

Maze 37

CABBAGE

Rated Time Limit | 40½ Minutes

Maze 38

THREAT

Rated Time Limit | 43 Minutes

Maze 39

OBESITY

Rated Time Limit | 43½ Minutes

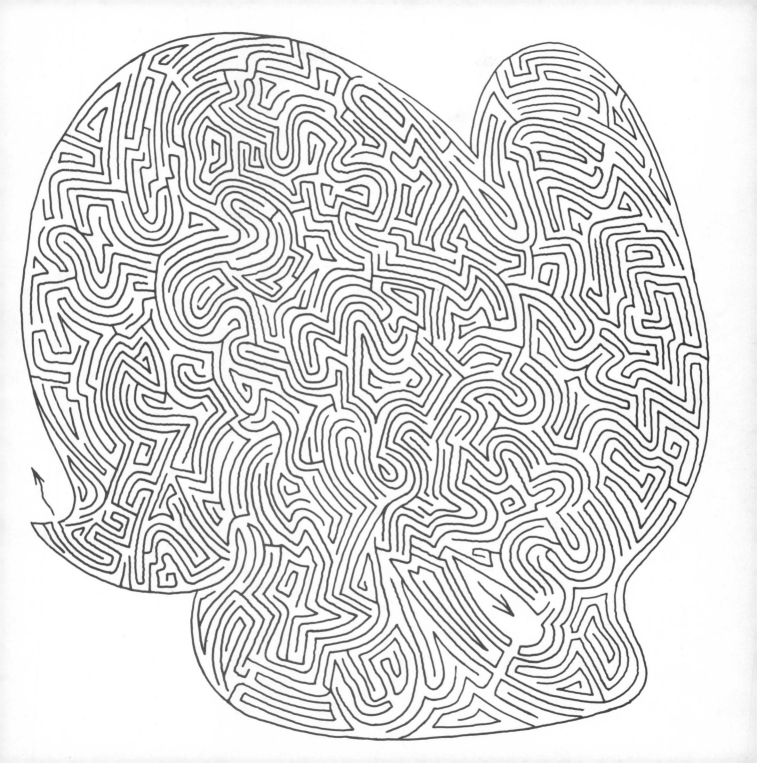

Maze 40
CLAUSTROPHOBIA
Rated Time Limit | 45 Minutes

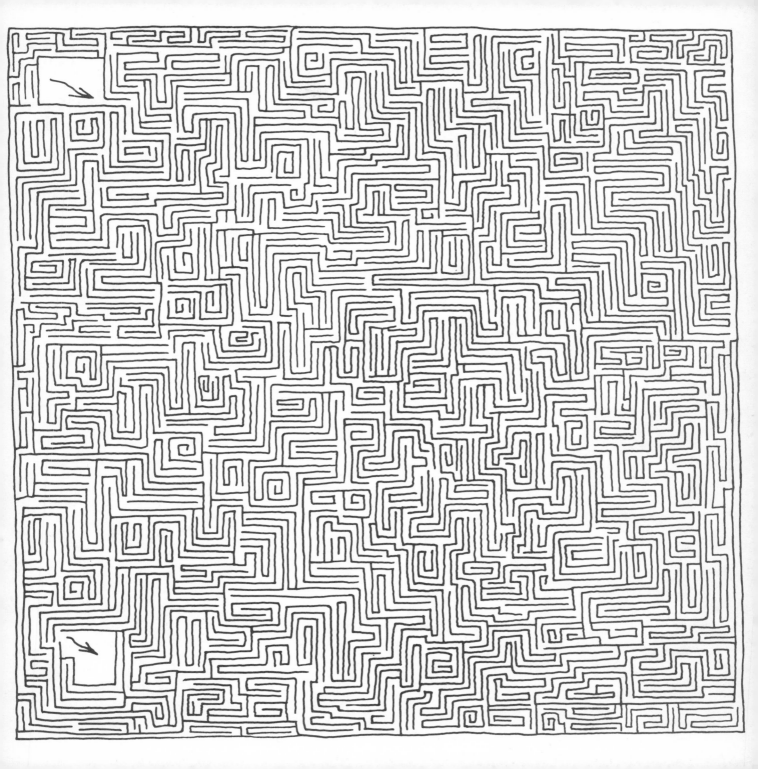

Solutions

Maze 1

Maze 2

Maze 3

Maze 4

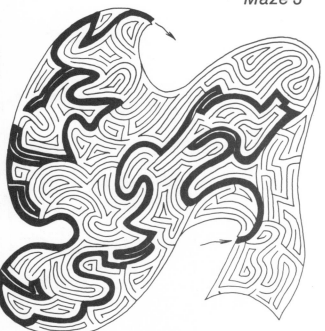

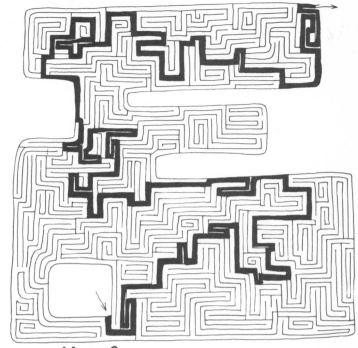

Maze 5

Maze 6

Maze 7

Maze 8

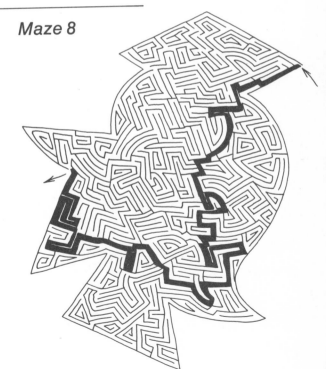

Maze 9

Maze 10

Maze 11

Maze 12

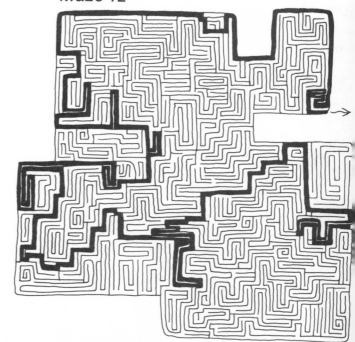

Maze 13

Maze 14

Maze 15

Maze 16

Maze 17

Maze 18

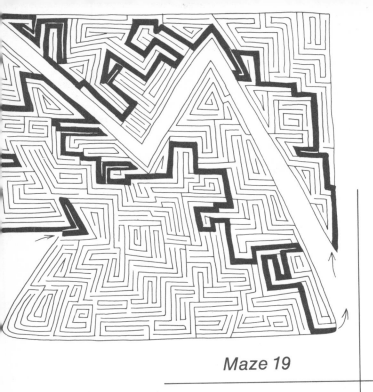

Maze 19

Maze 20

Maze 21

Maze 22

Maze 23

Maze 24

Maze 25

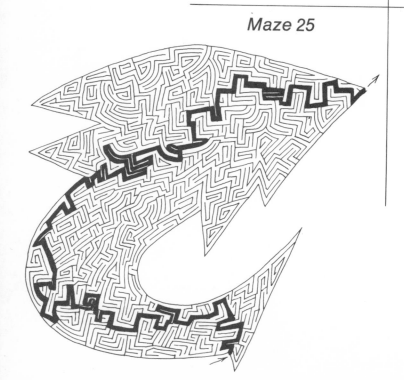

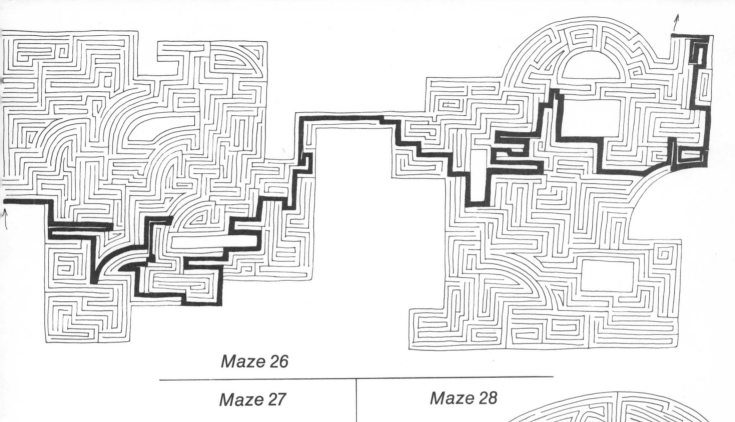

Maze 26

Maze 27　　　　Maze 28

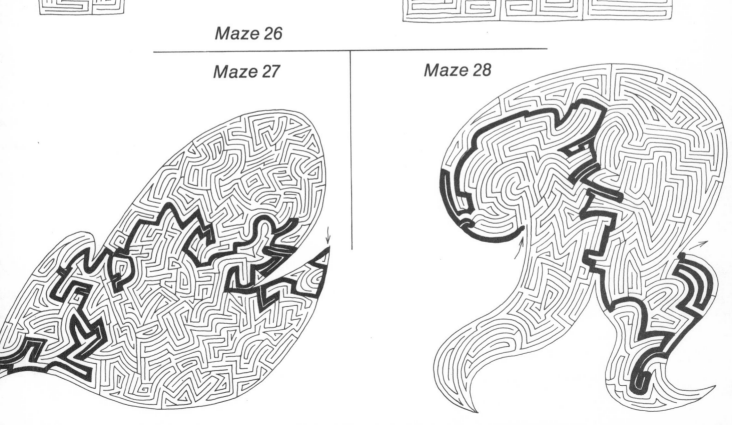

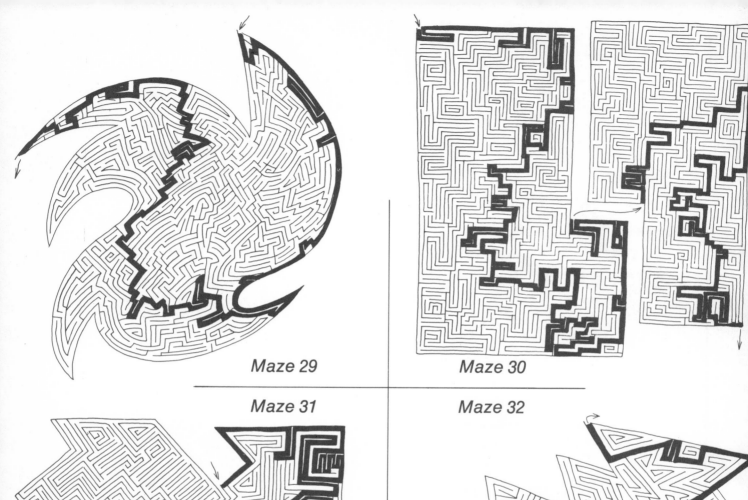

Maze 29

Maze 30

Maze 31

Maze 32

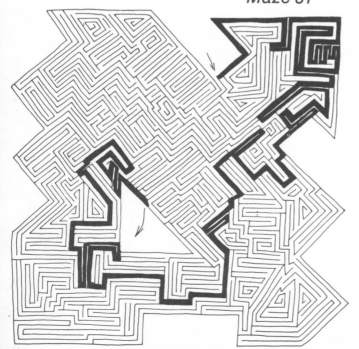

Maze 33

Maze 34

Maze 35

Maze 36

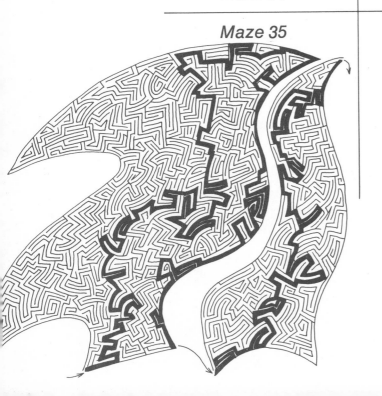

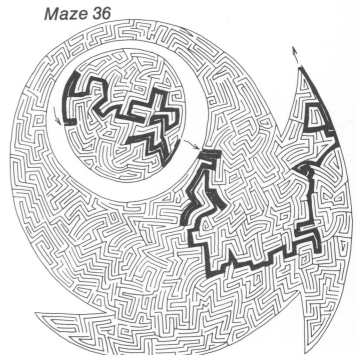

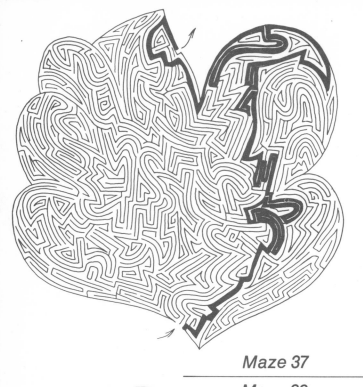

Maze 37

Maze 38

Maze 39

Maze 40

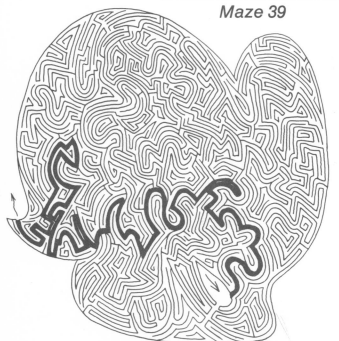

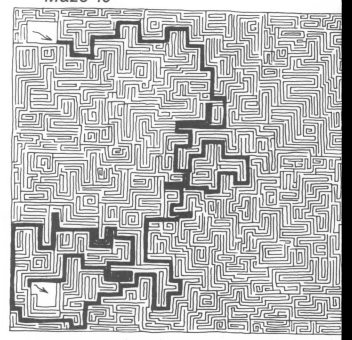